This England: A Treasury of Poems and Pictures

The Photographers

Kathleen Freeman
Louise Shakespeare
Clifford Shakespeare

Editor

Barry Freeman

Arrow Valley Publications

Arrow Valley Publications
Church Lane, Eardisland
Herefordshire HR6 9BP
Tel: 01544 388226

Printed by Print Plus: Hereford
Tel: 01432 272025

ISBN 0 9538081 1 4

ACKNOWLEDGEMENTS

Arrow Valley Publications gratefully acknowledges permission to reprint the following poems:

The Society of Authors: *The Holly*, Walter de la Mare; *Loveliest of Trees* and *Bredon Hill*, A. E. Housman; *Up On The Downs*, *The Waggon-Maker* and *Sea Fever*, John Masefield; *The Burning of Leaves*, Laurence Binyon.

Faber and Faber Ltd: *If I Could Tell You*, W. H. Auden; *Pennines in April*, Ted Hughes; *Zenner*, Anne Ridler.

John Murray (Publishers) Ltd: *A Subaltern's Love-Song*, *Diary of a Church Mouse* and *Trebetherick*, Sir John Betjeman.

A. P. Watt Ltd for The National Trust for Places of Historical Interest or Natural Beauty: *If*, *Tommy* and *The Glory of The Garden*, Rudyard Kipling.

Peters Fraser and Dunlop Group Ltd: *Miss Thompson Goes Shopping*, Martin Armstrong.

While every effort has been made to contact copyright holders, we apologise for any inadvertent omissions.

Front Cover: Cricket on The Green at Tilford, Surrey.
Opposite: Elstead Mill, Surrey.

The Poems

Page

8   John of Gaunt's Speech, William Shakespeare

10 I Wandered Lonely As A Cloud, William Wordsworth

12 Up On The Downs, John Masefield

15 English Character, George Crabbe

16 Weathers, Thomas Hardy

18 Home Thoughts From Abroad, Robert Browning

20 The Brook, Alfred, Lord Tennyson

22 Loveliest of Trees, A. E. Housman

24 Once More Unto The Breach, William Shakespeare

26 Elegy Written in a Country Churchyard, Thomas Grey

30 Adlestrop, Edward Thomas

32 Trebetherick, Sir John Betjeman

34 Pennines in April, Ted Hughes

36 Bluebells, George Barlow

38 To The Cockoo, William Wordsworth

40 The Waggon-Maker, John Masefield

42 Devon Glorious Devon, Sir Harold Boulton

45 If, Rudyard Kipling

46 Past and Present, Thomas Hood

48 The Soldier, Rupert Brooke

50 Ode On Solitude, Alexander Pope

53 Proposals For Building A Cottage, John Clare

54 The Rolling English Road, G. K. Chesterton

56 Bredon Hill, A. E. Housman

59 A Subaltern's Love-Song, Sir John Betjeman

60 Sea Fever, John Masefield

Page

62 Be not afeard, William Shakespeare

64 Grantchester, Rupert Brooke

68 Zennor, Anne Ridler

70 Amid the Barren Hills, Emily Brontë

70 Farewell, Anne Brontë

72 Winter In The Fens, John Clare

74 Tommy, Rudyard Kipling

76 Upon Westminster Bridge, William Wordsworth

78 Written At An Inn At Henley, William Shenstone

80 The Passionate Shepherd To His Love, Christopher Marlowe

82 Sonnet XVIII, William Shakespeare

84 Sudden Shower, John Clare

86 Ode to Autumn, John Keats

88 On Ploughing, Evelyn Bangay

91 The Holly, Walter de la Mare

92 The Oxen, Thomas Hardy

94 The Burning of Leaves, Laurence Binyon

97 Diary Of A Church Mouse, Sir John Betjeman

98 Miss Thompson Goes Shopping, Martin Armstrong

100 If I Could Tell You, W. H. Auden

102 Oxford, Tom Lovatt-Williams

104 Roundabouts And Swings, Patrick Chalmers

106 The Glory of The Garden, Rudyard Kipling

108 The Ruined Maid, Thomas Hardy

111 The Life That I Have, Leo Marks

113 The Gate Of The Year, M. Louise Haskins

The Pictures

LOUISE AND CLIFFORD SHAKESPEARE

Page

3 Elstead Mill, Surrey
9 Cottages at Cavendish, Suffolk
13 Where the Downs meet the sea
14 Sir Francis Drake. HMS Victory
17 Castle
19 Yorkshire
25 Arlington Row, Bibury, Gloucestershire
33 St Enodoc Church, Cornwall
35 Whitby
43 Waddeton village centre, Devon
44 Stokesay Castle, Shropshire
51 Rowing out to the yacht
52 John Clare's Cottage, Helpston
55 Ambling along a country road
58 Stained glass windows
61 Estuary near Dartmouth, Devon

63 West Bay, Dorset
65 Exeter College, Cambridge
67 Bridge of Sighs, Cambridge
69 St Agnes Head, Cornwall
73 Deep in the Fens
74 The thin red line
77 Westminster Bridge
83 In the poppy field
85 Unloading cockles at Wells, Norfolk
96 Selworthy Church, Somerset
99 Anticipation outside a cake shop, Lincoln
101 In the bleak midwinter
103 The High, Oxford
109 York: The Traditional English Tearooms
110 Sunset
112 Choristers at Peterborough Cathedral

KATHLEEN FREEMAN

Page

6 Eardisland in springtime
11 Discovering daffodils
21 A mountain stream
23 Blossomtime on Bringsty Common, Herefordshire
27 Broadwas Church, Worcestershire
29 Chapel at Dinmore Manor, Herefordshire
31 Upper Arley Station, Severn Valley Railway
37 Bluebells in woodland
39 Broadway, Worcestershire
41 Travellers' encampment
47 Thatched cottage at Eastnor, Herefordshire
49 Forever England
57 Summertime on Bredon Hill, Worcestershire

71 Castle Howard
79 On the Thames near Goring, Berkshire
81 Orchard in springtime
87 After the harvest
89 Ploughing with horses
90 Holly at Christmas
93 Silhouettes and shadows
95 Tending the bonfire
105 A giant of yesterday
107 Stone House garden, Worcestershire
114 Dovecotes in Gloucestershire and Herefordshire
115 Yat Rock, lower Wye valley
117 Olchon Valley, Herefordshire

Eardisland in springtime.

Introduction

England has been England for more than a thousand years, a point worth making at the dawn of a new millennium. During those long centuries, English writers have created the world's richest national literary heritage, and it is our poets who have become most deeply impressed upon our collective awareness.

Shakespeare was a poet: his one hundred and fifty-four sonnets are arguably the world's leading collection of poetry, not to mention his longer poems. He was also the most accomplished and prolific dramatist mankind has yet produced, and all his plays were written in verse.

Poetry, then, is etched into our minds. Snatches of speeches, lines from ballads, odd phrases from a random collection of poems. Frequently we misquote, forget the author, or the title, or what the next line is... but we are aware: aware of that wonderful heritage that our poets have bequeathed us down the centuries.

Poetry has become one of the essential defining elements of England and Englishness, and in turn it helps us to define other essential elements: character, landscape, the weather, seasons and emotions.

In this book I have sought to compile a collection of essentially English poems and then to complement them with a selection of equally English images. Here are the landscapes, buildings and people who most typify traditional England.

It has, we hear, become less than fashionable to be proud of England and our English heritage. There can be no greater mistake, for any nation, than to seek to erase history and heritage. They are what we have been, and created, during our nationhood, good and bad. Unless we value, conserve and study our intellectual and environmental legacy of the past millennium, we have no reliable chart to set a course into the coming centuries.

Inevitably any selection of poems must be strongly personal; influenced by one's awareness of and familiarity with certain poets and equally one's ignorance or lack of empathy with others. There are also constraints of space. I was looking for some fifty poems, not a thousand. Hopefully, however, everyone with a taste for traditional English poetry will find much to savour, recall and perhaps rediscover in this selection.

Here are the very well known indeed: the speech before Agincourt; Wordsworth remembering the galaxy of daffodils hanging above the lakeside and, in an entirely different setting, the view from Westminster Bridge; Keats with his 'season of mists and mellow fruitfulness' and Tennyson's brook tumbling down the mountainside.

There are two substantial poems; Grantchester, which I have always considered rather odd but felt must be included... the last two lines must be some of the most-quoted in the English language. Grey's Elegy is the other long poem, essential to any English anthology and again full of quoted verses, and it provided the title for one of Hardy's novels!

Kipling is here with three poems. He became denigrated some time back as a jingoistic Empire flag-waver. I have no qualms about including him and only feel sorry for those whose view of his output is so straitened.

In our village church we produce copies of some poems and put them on a table for sale. Copies of 'If' sell all the time: to young as well as old, foreign visitors as well as native English.

Finally, to one or two personal favourites; most of them I have cherished all my adult life. I am an incurable Betjemanian and have a row of books and videos to prove it! So he is here. Adlestrop is here too: it reminds me of journeys home from school at the end of term, on the Great Western, although it was British Rail by then. It also distils England in less than a hundred words.

Thank you, Edward Thomas, for Adlestrop. Thank you all for the poetry in this book. Thank you Thomas Hardy, for making me laugh every time I read The Ruined Maid. And lastly, a poignant thank you, to Anne Brontë for Farewell and Leo Marks for The Life That I have.

I do hope that you enjoy these poems and pictures.

Barry Freeman
Eardisland, September 2000.

From John of Gaunt's Speech

(RICHARD II, ACT II, SC I)

WILLIAM SHAKESPEARE

This royal throne of kings, this scepter'd isle,
This earth of majesty, this seat of Mars,
This other Eden, demi-paradise;
This fortress built by Nature for herself
Against infection and the hand of war;
This happy breed of men, this little world;
This precious stone set in a silver sea,
Which serves it in the office of a wall,
Or as a moat defensive to a house,
Against the envy of less happier lands;
This blessed plot, this earth, this realm, this England.

Cavendish, Suffolk.

I Wandered Lonely as a Cloud

WILLIAM WORDSWORTH

I wandered lonely as a cloud
That floats on high o'er vales and hills,
When all at once I saw a crowd,
A host, of golden daffodils;
Beside the lake, beneath the trees,
Fluttering and dancing in the breeze.

Continuous as the stars that shine
And twinkle on the milky way,
They stretched in never-ending line
Along the margin of a bay:
Ten thousand saw I at a glance,
Tossing their heads in sprightly dance.

The waves beside them danced; but they
Out-did the sparkling waves in glee:
A poet could not but be gay,
In such a jocund company:
I gazed – and gazed – but little thought
What wealth the show to me had brought:

For oft, when on my couch I lie
In vacant or in pensive mood,
They flash upon that inward eye
Which is the bliss of solitude:
And then my heart with pleasure fills,
And dances with the daffodils.

Opposite: Discovering daffodils

Up On The Downs

John Masefield

Up on the downs the red-eyed kestrels hover,
Eyeing the grass.
The field-mouse flits like a shadow into cover
As their shadows pass.

Men are burning the gorse on the down's shoulder;
A drift of smoke
Glitters with fire and hangs, and the skies smoulder,
And the lungs choke.

Once the tribe did thus on the downs, on these downs burning
Men in the frame,
Crying to the gods of the downs till their brains were turning
And the gods came.

And to-day on the downs, in the wind, the hawks, the grasses,
In blood and air,
Something passes me and cries as it passes,
On the chalk downland bare.

Where the downs meet the sea

English Character

GEORGE CRABBE

How stately stand yon pines upon the hill,
How soft the murmurs of that living rill,
And o'er the park's tall paling, scarcely higher,
Peeps the low Church and shows the modest spire.
Unnumber'd violets on those banks appear,
And all the first-born beauties of the year,
The grey-green blossoms of the willow bring
The large wild bees upon the labouring wing.
Then comes the Summer with augmented pride,
Whose pure small streams along the valleys glide:
Her richer Flora their brief charms display;
And, as the fruit advances, fall away.
Then shall th' autumnal yellow clothe the leaf,
What time the reaper binds the burden'd sheaf;
Then silent groves denote the dying year,
The morning frost, the noon-tide gossamer;
And all be silent in the scene around,
All save the distant sea's uncertain sound,
Or here and there the gun whose loud report
Proclaims to man that Death is but his sport;
And then the wintry winds begin to blow,
Then fall the flaky stars of gathering snow,
When on the thorn the ripening sloe, yet blue,
Takes the bright varnish of the morning dew;
The aged moss grows brittle on the pale,
The dry boughs splinter on the windy gale,
And every changing season of the year
Stamps on the scene its English character.

Opposite left: Sir Francis Drake, Plymouth
right: HMS Victory, Portsmouth

Weathers

Thomas Hardy

This is the weather the cuckoo likes,
    And so do I:
When showers betumble the chestnut spikes,
    And nestlings fly;
And the little brown nightingale bills his best,
And they sit outside at 'The Travellers' Rest',
And maids come forth sprig-muslin drest,
And citizens dream of the south and west,
    And so do I.

This is the weather the shepherd shuns.
    And so do I;
When beeches drip in browns and duns,
    And thresh, and ply;
And hill-hid tides throb, throe on throe,
And meadow rivulets overflow,
And drops on gate-bars hang in a row,
And rooks in families homeward go,
    And so do I.

Dunstanburgh Castle, Northumberland

Home Thoughts, from Abroad

ROBERT BROWNING

Oh, to be in England,
Now that April's there,
And whoever wakes in England
Sees, some morning, unaware,
That the lowest boughs and the brushwood sheaf
Round the elm-tree bole are in tiny leaf,
While the chaffinch sings on the orchard bough
In England – now!
And after April, when May follows,
And the whitethroat builds, and all the swallows!
Hark, where my blossomed pear-tree in the hedge
Leans to the field and scatters on the clover
Blossoms and dewdrops – at the bent spray's edge –
That's the wise thrush; he sings his song twice over,
Lest you should think he never could recapture
The first fine careless rapture!
And though the fields look rough with hoary dew,
All will be gay when noontide wakes anew
The buttercups, the little children's dower
– Far brighter than this gaudy melon-flower!

Helmsley. North Yorkshire.

The Brook

ALFRED, LORD TENNYSON

I come from haunts of coot and hern,
I make a sudden sally,
And sparkle out among the fern,
To bicker down a valley.

By thirty hills I hurry down,
Or slip between the ridges,
By twenty thorps, a little town,
And half a hundred bridges.

Till last by Philip's farm I flow
To join the brimming river,
For men may come and men may go
But I go on for ever.

I chatter over stony ways,
In little sharps and trebles,
I bubble into eddying bays,
I babble on the pebbles.

With many a curve my banks I fret
By many a field and fallow,
And many a fairy foreland set
With willow-weed and mallow.

I chatter, chatter, as I flow
To join the brimming river,
For men may come and men may go,
But I go on for ever.

I wind about, and in and out,
With here a blossom sailing,
And here and there a lusty trout,
And here and there a grayling.

And here and there a foamy flake
Upon me, as I travel
With many a silvery waterbreak
Above the golden gravel,

And draw them all along, and flow
To join the brimming river,
For men may come and men may go,
But I go on for ever.

I steal by lawns and grassy plots,
I slide by hazel covers;
I move the sweet forget-me-nots
That grow for happy lovers.

I slip, I slide, I gloom, I glance,
Among my skimming swallows;
I make the netted sunbeam dance
Against my sandy shallows.

I murmur under moon and stars
In brambly wildernesses;
I linger by my shingly bars;
I loiter round my cresses.

And out again I curve and flow
To join the brimming river,
For men may come and men may go,
But I go on for ever.

A mountain stream.

Loveliest of Trees

From *A Shropshire Lad*

A E Housman

Loveliest of trees, the cherry now
Is hung with bloom along the bough,
And stands about the woodland ride
Wearing white for Eastertide.

Now, of my threescore years and ten,
Twenty will not come again,
And take from seventy springs a score,
It only leaves me fifty more.

And since to look at things in bloom
Fifty springs are little room,
About the woodlands I will go
To see the cherry hung with snow.

Opposite: Blossom time on Bringsty Common, Herefordshire.

William Shakespeare

FROM HENRY IV, ACT III Sc 1

Once more unto the breach, dear friends, once more;
Or close the wall up with our English dead!
In peace there's nothing so becomes a man
As modest stillness and humility:
But when the blast of war blows in our ears,
Then imitate the action of the tiger;
Stiffen the sinews, summon up blood,
Disguise fair nature with hard-favour'd rage;
Then lend the eye a terrible aspect;
Let it pry through the portage of the head
Like the brass cannon; let the brow o'erwhelm it
As fearfully as doth a galled rock
O'erhang and jutty his confounded base,
Swill'd with the wild and wasteful ocean.
Now set the teeth and stretch the nostril wide,
Hold hard the breath, and bend up every spirit
To his full height! On, on, you noblest English!
Whose blood is fet from fathers of war-proof;
Fathers that, like so many Alexanders,

Have in these parts from morn til even fought,
And sheath'd their swords for lack of argument.
Dishonour not your mothers; now attest
That those whom you call'd fathers did beget
you.
Be copy now to men of grosser blood.
And teach them how to war. And you, good
yeomen,
Whose limbs were made in England, show us
here
The mettle of your pasture; let us swear
That you are worth your breeding; which I
doubt not;
For there is none of you so mean and base
That hath not noble lustre in your eyes.
I see you stand like greyhounds in the slips,
Straining upon the start. The game's afoot:
Follow your spirit; and, upon this charge
Cry 'God for Harry! England and Saint George!'

Arlington Row, Bibury, Gloucestershire.

Elegy Written in a Country Churchyard

Thomas Gray

The curfew tolls the knell of parting day,
The lowing herd winds slowly o'er the lea,
The ploughman homeward plods his weary way,
And leaves the world to darkness and to me.

Now fades the glimmering landscape on the sight,
And all the air a solemn stillness holds,
Save where the beetle wheels his droning flight,
And drowsy tinklings lull the distant folds;

Save that from yonder ivy-mantled tower
The moping owl does to the moon complain
Of such as, wandering near her secret bower,
Molest her ancient solitary reign.

Beneath those rugged elms, that yew-tree's shade,
Where heaves the turf in many a mouldering heap,
Each in his narrow cell for ever laid,
The rude forefathers of the hamlet sleep.

The breezy call of incense-breathing morn,
The swallow twittering from the straw-built shed,
The cock's shrill clarion or the echoing horn,
No more shall rouse them from their lowly bed.

For them no more the blazing hearth shall burn,
Or busy housewife ply her evening care:
No children run to lisp their sire's return,
Or climb his knees the envied kiss to share.

Oft did the harvest to their sickle yield,
Their furrow oft the stubborn glebe has broke:
How jocund did they drive their team afield!
How bowed the woods beneath their sturdy stroke!

Let not Ambition mock their useful toil,
Their homely joys and destiny obscure;
Nor Grandeur hear, with a disdainful smile,
The short and simple annals of the poor.

The boast of heraldry, the pomp of power,
And all that beauty, all that wealth e'er gave,
Awaits alike the inevitable hour.
The paths of glory lead but to the grave.

Nor you, ye Proud, impute to these the fault,
If Memory o'er their tomb no trophies raise,
Where through the long-drawn aisle and fretted vault
The pealing anthem swells the note of praise.

Can storied urn or animated bust
Back to its mansion call the fleeting breath?
Can Honour's voice provoke the silent dust,
Or Flattery soothe the dull cold ear of Death?

Perhaps in this neglected spot is laid
Some heart once pregnant with celestial fire;
Hands that the rod of empire might have swayed,
Or waked to ecstacy the living lyre.

But Knowledge to their eyes her ample page
Rich with the spoils of time did ne'er unroll;
Chill Penury repressed their noble rage,
And froze the genial current of the soul.

Full many a gem of purest ray serene
The dark unfathomed caves of ocean bear:
Full many a flower is born to blush unseen,
And waste its sweetness on the desert air.

Some village-Hampden that with dauntless breast
The little tyrant of his fields withstood;
Some mute inglorious Milton here may rest,
Some Cromwell guiltless of his country's blood.

The applause of listening senates to command,
The threats of pain and ruin to despise,
To scatter plenty o'er a smiling land,
And read their history in a nation's eyes.

Their lot forbade; nor circumscribed alone
Their growing virtues, but their crimes confined;
Forbade to wade through slaughter to a throne,
And shut the gates of mercy on mankind,

The struggling pangs of conscious truth to hide,
To quench the blushes of ingenuous shame,
Or heap the shrine of Luxury and Pride
With incense kindled at the Muse's flame.

Far from the madding crowd's ignoble strife
Their sober wishes never learned to stray;
Along the cool sequestered vale of life
They kept the noiseless tenor of their way.

Yet even these bones from insult to protect
Some frail memorial still erected nigh,
With uncouth rhymes and shapeless sculpture decked,
Implores the passing tribute of a sigh.

Broadwas Church, Worcestershire

Their name, their years, spelt by the unlettered muse,
The place of fame and elegy supply:
And many a holy text around she strews,
That teach the rustic moralist to die.

For who to dumb Forgetfulness a prey,
This pleasing anxious being e'er resigned,
Left the warm precincts of the cheerful day,
Nor cast one longing lingering look behind?

On some fond breast the parting soul relies,
Some pious drops the closing eye requires;
Even from the tomb the voice of Nature cries,
Even in our ashes live their wonted fires.

For thee who, mindful of the unhonoured dead,
Dost in these lines their artless tale relate;
If chance, by lonely Contemplation led,
Some kindred spirit shall inquire thy fate.

Haply some hoary-headed swain may say,
'Oft have we seen him at the peep of dawn
Brushing with hasty steps the dews away
To meet the sun upon the upland lawn.

'There at the foot of yonder nodding beech
That wreathes its old fantastic roots so high,
His listless length at noontide would he stretch,
And pore upon the brook that babbles by.

'Hard by yon wood, now smiling as in scorn,
Muttering his wayward fancies he would rove,
Now drooping, woeful wan, like one forlorn,
Or crazed with care, or crossed in hopeless love.

'One morn I missed him on the customed hill,
Along the heath and near his favourite tree;
Another came; nor yet beside the rill,
Nor up the lawn, nor at the wood was he;

'The next with dirges due in sad array
Slow through the church-way path we saw him borne.
Approach and read (for thou canst read) the lay,
Graved on the stone beneath yon aged thorn.'

The Epitaph

Here rests his head upon the lap of earth
A youth to Fortune and to Fame unknown.
Fair Science frowned not on his humble birth,
And Melancholy marked him for her own.

Large was his bounty and his soul sincere,
Heaven did a recompense as largely send:
He gave to Misery all he had, a tear,
He gained from Heaven ('twas all he wished) a friend.

No farther seek his merits to disclose,
Or draw his frailties from their dread abode,
(There they alike in trembling hope repose)
The bosom of his Father and his God.

Chapel at Dinmore Manor, Herefordshire.

Adlestrop

EDWARD THOMAS

Yes, I remember Adlestrop –
The name, because one afternoon
Of heat the express-train drew up there
Unwontedly. It was late June.

The steam hissed. Someone cleared his throat
No one left and no one came
On the bare platform. What I saw
Was Adlestrop – only the name.

And willows, willow-herb, and grass,
And meadowsweet, and haycocks dry,
No whit less still and lonely fair
Than the high cloudlets in the sky.

And for that minute a blackbird sang
Close by, and round him, mistier,
Farther and farther, all the birds
Of Oxfordshire and Gloucestershire.

Op[posite: Upper Arley, Severn Valley Railway.

Trebetherick

John Betjeman

We used to picnic where the thrift
    Grew deep and tufted to the edge:
We saw the yellow foam-flakes drift
    In trembling sponges on the ledge
Below us, till the wind would lift
    Them up the cliff and o'er the hedge.
Sand in the sandwiches, wasps in the tea,
Sun on our bathing-dresses heavy with the wet,
Squelch of the bladder-wrack waiting for the sea,
Fleas round the tamarisk, an early cigarette.

From where the coastguard houses stood
    One used to see, below the hill,
The lichened branches of a wood
    In summer silver-cool and still;
And there the Shade of Evil could
    Stretch out at us from Shilla Mill.
Thick with sloe and blackberry, uneven in the light,
Lonely ran the hedge, the heavy meadow was remote,
The oldest part of Cornwall was the wood as black as night,
And the pheasant and the rabbit lay torn open at the throat.

But when a storm was at its height,
    And feathery slate was black in rain.
And tamarisks were hung with light
    And golden sand was brown again,
Spring tide and blizzard would unite
    And sea came flooding up the lane.
Waves full of treasure then were roaring up the beach,
Ropes round our mackintoshes, waders warm and dry,
We waited for the wreckage to come swirling into reach,
Ralph, Vasey, Alastair, Biddy, John and I.

Then roller into roller curled
    And thundered down the rocky bay,
And we were in a water-world
    Of rain and blizzard, sea and spray,
And one against the other hurled
    We struggled round to Greenaway.
Blessèd be St Enodoc, blessèd be the waves,
Blessèd be the springy turf, we pray, pray to thee,
Ask for our children all the happy days you gave
To Ralph, Vasey, Alastair, Biddy, John and me.

St Enodoc Church, Cornwall.

Pennines in April

Ted Hughes

If this country were a sea (that is solid rock
Deeper than any sea) these hills heaving
Out of the east, mass behind mass, at this height
Hoisting heather and stones to the sky
Must burst upwards and topple into Lancashire.

Perhaps, as the earth turns, such ground-stresses
Do come rolling westward through the locked land.
Now, measuring the miles of silence
Your eye takes the strain: through

Landscapes gliding blue as water
Those barrellings of strength are heaving slowly and heave
To your feet and surf upwards
In a still, fiery air, hauling the imagination,
Carrying the larks upwards.

Whitby.

34

Bluebells

GEORGE BARLOW

'One day, one day, I'll climb that distant hill
    And pick the bluebells there!'
So dreamed the child who lived beside the rill
And breathed the lowland air
    'One day, one day when I am old I'll go
And climb the mountain where the bluebells blow.'

'One day! one day!' The child was now a maid,
 A girl with laughing look;
She and her lover sought the valley-glade
Where sang the silver brook.
 'One day,' she said, 'love, you and I will go
And reach that far hill where the bluebells blow!'

Years passed. A woman now with wearier eyes
 Gazed towards that sunlit hill.
Tall children clustered round her. How time flies!
The bluebells blossomed still.
 She'll never gather them! All dreams fade so.
We live and die, and still the bluebells blow.

Bluebells in woodland.

To the Cuckoo

WILLIAM WORDSWORTH

O blithe New-comer! I have heard,
I hear thee and rejoice.
O Cuckoo! shall I call thee Bird,
Or but a wandering Voice?

While I am lying on the grass
Thy twofold shout I hear,
From hill to hill it seems to pass,
At once far off, and near.

Though babbling only to the Vale,
Of sunshine and of flowers,
Thou bringest unto me a tale
Of visionary hours.

Thrice welcome, darling of the Spring!
Even yet thou art to me
No bird, but an invisible thing,
A voice, a mystery;

The same whom in my school-boy days
I listened to; that Cry
Which made me look a thousand ways
In bush, and tree, and sky.

To seek thee did I often rove
Through woods and on the green;
And thou wert still a hope, a love;
Still longed for, never seen.

And I can listen to thee yet;
Can lie upon the plain
And listen, till I do beget
That golden time again,

O blessèd Bird! the earth we pace
Again appears to be
An unsubstantial, faery place;
That is fit home for Thee!

Opposite: Broadway, Worcestershire.

The Waggon-Maker

John Masefield

I have made tales in verse, but this man made
Waggons of elm to last a hundred years;
The blacksmith forged the rims and iron gears,
His was the magic that the wood obeyed.

Each deft device that country wisdom bade,
Of farmers' practice needed, he preserved.
He wrought the subtle contours, straight and curved,
Only by eye, and instinct of the trade.

No weakness, no offence in any part,
It stood the strain in mired fields and roads
In all a century's struggle for its bread;
Bearing, perhaps, eight thousand heavy loads.
Beautiful always as a work of art,
Homing the bride, and harvest, and men dead.

Opposite: A travellers' encampment.

Devon, Glorious Devon

Sir Harold Boulton

Coombe and Tor, green meadow and lane,
Birds on the waving bough,
Beetling cliffs by the surging main,
Rich red loam for the plough;
Devon's the fount of the bravest blood
That braces England's breed;
Her maidens fair as the apple bud,
And her men are men indeed.

> When Adam and Eve were dispossesed
> Of the Garden hard by Heaven,
> They planted another one down in the West
> 'Twas Devon – 'twas Devon ...
> *Glorious Devon!*

Dorset, Somerset, Cornwall, Wales,
May envy the likes of we,
For the flow'r of the West, the first, the best,
The pick of the bunch us be.
Squab pie, junket, and cyder brew,
Richest of cream from the cow,
What 'ud old England without 'em do?
And where 'ud 'un be to now?

> As crumpy as a lump of lead
> Be a loaf without good leaven,
> And the yeast Mother England do use for her bread
> Be Devon – be Devon ...
> *Glorious Devon!*

Spirits of old-world heroes wake,
By river and cove and hoe –
Grenville, Hawkins, Raleigh and Drake,
And a thousand more we know.
To every land the wide world o'er
Some slips of the old stock roam;
Loyal friends in peace, dread foes in war,
With hearts still true to home.

> Old England's counties by the sea
> From East to West are seven
> But the gem of that fair galaxy
> Is Devon – is Devon ...
> *Glorious Devon!*

Waddeton, Devon.

42

If

Rudyard Kipling

If you can keep your head when all about you
  Are losing theirs and blaming it on you;
If you can trust yourself when all men doubt you,
  But make allowance for their doubting too;
If you can wait and not be tired by waiting,
  Or being lied about, don't deal in lies,
Or being hated don't give way to hating,
  And yet don't look too good, nor talk too wise

If you can dream – and not make dreams your master;
  If you can think – and not make thoughts your aim;
If you can meet with Triumph and Disaster
  And treat those two imposters just the same;
If you can bear to hear the truth you've spoken
  Twisted by knaves to make a trap for fools,
Or watch the things you gave your life to broken,
  And stoop and build 'em up with worn-out tools.

If you can make one heap of all your winnings
  And risk it on one turn of pitch-and-toss,
And lose, and start again at your beginnings
  And never breathe a word about your loss;
If you can force your heart and nerve and sinew
  To serve your turn long after they are gone,
And so hold on when there is nothing in you
  Except the Will which says to them: "Hold on!"

If you can talk with crowds and keep your virtue
  Or walk with Kings – nor lose the common touch,
If neither foes nor loving friends can hurt you,
  If all men count with you, but none too much;
If you can fill the unforgiving minute
  With sixty seconds' worth of distance run,
Yours is the Earth and everything that's in it,
  And – which is more – you'll be a Man, my son!

Stokesay Castle, Shropshire.

Past and Present

Thomas Hood

I remember, I remember
The house where I was born,
The little window where the sun
Came peeping in at morn;
He never came a wink too soon,
Nor brought too long a day;
But now, I often wished the night
Had borne my breath away.

I remember, I remember
The roses, red and white,
The violets, and the lily-cups –
Those flowers made of light!
The lilacs where the robin built,
And where my brother set
The laburnum on his birth-day, –
The tree is living yet!

I remember, I remember
Where I was used to swing,
And thought the air must rush as fresh
To swallows on the wing;
My spirit flew in feathers then
That is so heavy now,
And summer pools could hardly cool
The fever on my brow.

I remember, I remember
The fir trees dark and high;
I used to think their slender tops
Were close against the sky:
It was a childish ignorance,
But now 'tis little joy
To know I'm farther off from Heaven
Than when I was a boy.

Cottage at Eastnor, Herefordshire.

The Soldier

RUPERT BROOKE

If I should die think only this of me:
That there's some corner of a foreign field
That is for ever England. There shall be
In that rich earth a richer dust concealed;
A dust whom England bore, shaped, made aware,
Gave, once, her flowers to love, her ways to roam.
A body of England's, breathing English air,
Washed by the rivers, blest by suns of home.

And think, this heart, all evil shed away,
A pulse in the eternal mind, no less
Gives somewhere back the thoughts by England given;
Her sights and sounds; dreams happy as her day;
And laughter, learnt of friends; and gentleness,
In hearts at peace, under an English heaven.

Forever England.

48

Ode on Solitude

ALEXANDER POPE

Happy the man, whose wish and care
A few paternal acres bound,
Content to breathe his native air
    In his own ground.

Whose herds with milk, whose fields with bread,
Whose flocks supply him with attire:
Whose trees in summer yield him shade
    In winter, fire.

Blest, who can unconcern'dly find
Hours, days, and years, slide soft away
In health of body, peace of mind,
    Quiet by day.

Sound sleep by night; study and ease
Together mixt, sweet recreation,
And innocence, which most does please
    With meditation.

Thus let me live, unseen, unknown;
Thus unlamented let me die;
Steal from the world, and not a stone
    Tell where I lie.

Rowing out to the yacht.

After Reading in a Letter Proposals for Building a Cottage

JOHN CLARE

Beside a runnel build my shed,
   With stubbles covered o'er;
Let broad oaks o'er its chimney spread,
   And grass-plats grace the door.

The door may open with a string,
   So that it closes tight;
And locks would be a wanted thing,
   To keep out thieves at night.

A little garden, not too fine,
   Inclose with painted pales;
And woodbines, round the cot to twine,
   Pin to the wall with nails.

Let hazels grow, and spindling sedge,
   Bend bowering over-head;
Dig old man's beard from woodland hedge,
   To twine a summer shade.

Beside the threshold sods provide,
   And build a summer seat;
Plant sweet-briar bushes by its side,
   And flowers that blossom sweet.

I love the sparrow's ways to watch
   Upon the cotter's sheds,
So here and there pull out the thatch,
   That they might hide their heads.

And as the sweeping swallows stop
   Their flights along the green,
Leave holes within the chimney-top
   To paste their nest between.

Stick shelves and cupboards round the hut,
   In all the holes and nooks;
Nor in the corner fail to put
   A cupboard for the books.

Along the floor some sand I'll shift,
   To make it fit to live in;
And then I'll thank ye for the gift,
   As something worth the giving.

THIS MEMORIAL
IS ERECTED TO PERPETUATE
THE MEMORY OF
JOHN CLARE,
THE NORTHAMPTONSHIRE
PEASANT POET
A NATIVE OF THIS VILLAGE
BORN JULY 13TH 1793 DIED MAY 20TH 1864.

Opposite: John Clare's cottage, Helpston.

The Rolling English Road

G K Chesterton

Before the Roman came to Rye or out to Severn strode,
The rolling English drunkard made the rolling English road.
A reeling road, a rolling road, that rambles round the shire,
And after him the parson ran, the sexton and the squire;
A merry road, a mazy road, and such as we did tread
The night we went to Birmingham by way of Beachy Head.

I knew no harm of Bonaparte and plenty of the Squire,
And for to fight the Frenchman I did not much desire;
But I did bash their baggonets because they came arrayed
To straighten out the crooked road an English drunkard made,
Where you and I went down the lane with ale-mugs in our hands,
The night we went to Glastonbury by way of Goodwin Sands.

His sins they were forgiven him; or why do flowers run
Behind him; and the hedges all strengthening in the sun?
The wild thing went from left to right and knew not which was which,
But the wild rose was above him when they found him in the ditch.
God pardon us, nor harden us; we did not see so clear
The night we went to Bannockburn by way of Brighton Pier.

My friends, we will not go again or ape an ancient rage,
Or stretch the folly of our youth to be the shame of age,
But walk with clearer eyes and ears this path that wandereth,
And see undrugged in evening light the decent inn of death;
For there is good news yet to hear and fine things to be seen,
Before we go to Paradise by way of Kensal Green.

Ambling along a country road.

Bredon Hill

FROM *A SHROPSHIRE LAD*

A E HOUSMAN

In summertime on Bredon
  The bells they sound so clear;
Round both the shires they ring them
  In steeples far and near,
  A happy noise to hear.

Here of a Sunday morning
  My love and I would lie,
And see the coloured counties,
  And hear the larks so high
  About us in the sky.

The bells would ring to call her
  In valleys miles away:
'Come all to church, good people;
  Good people, come and pray.'
  But here my love would stay.

And I would turn and answer
  Among the springing thyme,
'Oh, peal upon our wedding,
  And we will hear the chime
  And come to church in time.'

But when the snows at Christmas
  On Bredon top were strown,
My love rose up so early
  And stole out unbeknown
  And went to church alone

They tolled the one bell only,
  Groom there was none to see,
The mourners followed after,
  And so to church went she,
  And would not wait for me.

The bells they sound on Bredon,
  And still the steeples hum.
'Come all to church, good people,' –
  Oh, noisy bells, be dumb;
  I hear you, I will come.

Summertime on Bredon Hill, Worcestershire.

In Cruce Salus

A Subaltern's Love-Song

Sir John Betjeman

Miss J Hunter Dunn, Miss J Hunter Dunn,
Furnish'd and burnish'd by Aldershot sun.
What strenuous singles we played after tea,
We in the tournament – you against me!

Love-thirty, love-forty, oh! weakness of joy,
The speed of a swallow, the grace of a boy,
With carefullest carelessness, gaily you won,
I am weak from your loveliness, Joan Hunter Dunn.

Miss Joan Hunter Dunn, Miss Joan Hunter Dunn,
How mad I am, sad I am, glad that you won.
The warm-handled racket is back in its press,
But my shock-headed victor, she loves me no less.

Her father's euonymus shines as we walk,
And swing past the summer-house, buried in talk,
And cool the verandah that welcomes us in
To the six-o'clock news and a lime-juice and gin.

The scent of the conifers, sound of the bath,
The view from my bedroom of moss-dappled path,
As I struggle with double-end evening tie,
For we dance at the Golf Club, my victor and I.

On the floor of her bedroom lie blazer and shorts
And the cream-coloured walls are be-trophied with sports,
And westering, questioning settles the sun
On your low-leaded window, Miss Joan Hunter Dunn.

The Hillman is waiting, the light's in the hall,
The pictures of Egypt are bright on the wall,
My sweet, I am standing beside the oak stair
And there on the landing's the light on your hair.

By roads 'not adopted', by woodlanded ways,
She drove to the club in the late summer haze,
Into nine-o'clock Camberley, heavy with bells,
And mushroomy, pine-woody, evergreen smells.

Miss Joan Hunter Dunn, Miss Joan Hunter Dunn,
I can hear from the car-park the dance has begun.
Oh! full Surrey twilight! importunate band!
Oh! strongly adorable tennis-girl's hand!

Around us are Rovers and Austins afar,
Above us, the intimate roof of the car,
And here on my right is the girl of my choice,
With the tilt of her nose and the chime of her voice.

And the scent of her wrap, and the words never said,
And the ominous, ominous dancing ahead.
We sat in the car-park till twenty to one
And now I'm engaged to Miss Joan Hunter Dunn.

Stained glass windows at Appledore(l) and Bury St Edmonds(r)

Sea-Fever

John Masefield

I must go down to the seas again, to the lonely sea and the sky,
And all I ask is a tall ship and a star to steer her by,
And the wheel's kick and the wind's song and the white sail's shaking,
And a grey mist on the sea's face and a grey dawn breaking.

I must go down to the seas again, for the call of the running tide,
Is a wild call and a clear call that may not be denied;
And all I ask is a windy day with the white clouds flying,
And the flung spray and the blown spume, and the sea-gulls crying.

I must go down to the seas again, to the vagrant gypsy life,
To the gull's way and the whale's way where the wind's like a whetted knife;
And all I ask is a merry yarn from a laughing fellow-rover,
And a quiet sleep and a sweet dream when the long trick's over.

Estuary near Dartmouth.

The Isle is full of noises...

WILLIAM SHAKESPEARE

FROM THE TEMPEST ACT III SC II

Be not afeard: the isle is full of noises,
Sounds and sweet airs, that give delight, and hurt not.
Sometimes a thousand twangling instruments
Will hum about mine ears; and sometimes voices,
That, if I then had wak'd after long sleep,
Will make me sleep again: and then, in dreaming,
The clouds methought would open and show riches
Ready to drop upon me; that, when I wak'd
I cried to dream again.

West Bay, Dorset

The Old Vicarage, Grantchester

RUPERT BROOKE

Just now the lilac is in bloom,
All before my little room;
And in my flower beds, I think,
Smile the carnation and the pink;
And down the borders, well I know;
The poppy and the pansy blow ...
Oh! there the chestnuts, summer through,
Beside the river make for you
A tunnel of green gloom, and sleep
Deeply above; and green and deep
The stream mysterious glides beneath,
Green as a dream and deep as death.
– Oh, damn! I know it! and I know
How the May fields all golden show,
And when the day is young and sweet,
Gild gloriously the bare feet
That run to bathe ...
    Du lieber Gott!

Here am I, sweating, sick and hot,
And there the shadowed waters fresh
Lean to embrace the naked flesh.
Temperamentvoll German Jews
Drink beer around – and *there* the dews
Are soft beneath a morn of gold.
Here tulips bloom as they are told;
Unkempt about those hedges blows
An English unofficial rose;
And there the unregulated sun
Slopes down to rest when day is done,
And wakes a vague unpunctual star,
A slippered Hesper; and there are
Meads towards Haslingfield and Coton
Where *das Betreten*'s not *verboten*.

Εἴθε γενοίμην ... Would I were
In Grantchester, in Grantchester!
Some, it may be, can get in touch
With Nature there, or Earth, or such.
And clever modern men have seen
A Faun a-peeping through the green,
And felt the Classics were not dead.
To glimpse a Naiad's reedy head.
Or hear the Goat-foot piping low: ...
But these are things I do not know.
I only know that you may lie
Day-long and watch the Cambridge sky,
And, flower-lulled in sleepy grass,
Hear the cool lapse of hours pass,
Until the centuries blend and blurr

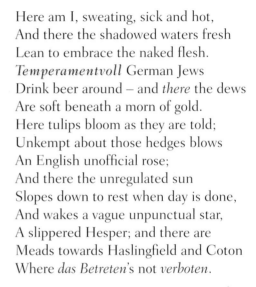

In Grantchester, in Grantchester ...
Still in the dawnlit waters cool
His ghostly Lordship swims his pool,
And tries the strokes, essays the tricks,
Long learnt on Hellespont, or Styx.
Dan Chaucer hears his river still
Chatter beneath a phantom mill.
Tennyson notes, with studious eye,
How Cambridge waters hurry by ...
And in that garden, black and white,
Creep whispers through the grass all night;
And spectral dance, before the dawn,
A hundred Vicars down the lawn:
Curates, long dust, will come and go
On lissom, clerical, printless toe;
And oft between the boughs is seen
The sly shade of a Rural Dean ...
Till, at a shiver in the skies,
Vanishing with Satanic cries,
The prim ecclesiastic rout
Leaves but a startled sleeper-out.
Grey heavens, the first bird's drowsy calls,
The falling house that never falls.

God! I will pack, and take a train,
And get me to England once again!
For England's the one land, I know,
Where men with Splendid Hearts may go;
And Cambridgeshire, of all England,
The shire for Men who Understand;
And of *that* district I prefer
The lovely hamlet Grantchester.

Exeter College, Cambridge.

For Cambridge people rarely smile,
Being urban, squat, and packed with guile;
And Royston men in the far South
Are black and fierce and strange of mouth;
At Over they fling oaths at one,
And worse than oaths at Trumpington,
And Ditton girls are mean and dirty,
And there's none in Harston under thirty,
And folks in Shelford and those parts
Have twisted lips and twisted hearts.
And Barton men make Cockney rhymes,
And Coton's full of nameless crimes.
And things are done you'd not believe
At Madingley, on Christmas Eve,
Strong men have run for miles and miles,
When one from Cherry Hinton smiles;
Strong men have blanched, and shot their wives,
Rather than send them to St Ives;
Strong men have cried like babes, bydam,
To hear what happened at Babraham.
But Grantchester! ah, Grantchester!
There's peace and holy quiet there,
Great clouds along pacific skies,
And men and women with straight eyes,
Lithe children lovelier than a dream,
A bosky wood, a slumbrous stream,
And little kindly winds that creep
Round twilight corners, half asleep.
In Grantchester their skins are white;
They bathe by day, they bathe by night;
The women there do all they ought;
The men observe the Rules of Thought.

They love the Good; they worship Truth;
They laugh uproariously in youth;
(And when they get to feeling old,
They up and shoot themselves, I'm told) ,,,

Ah God! to see the branches stir
Across the moon at Grantchester!
To smell the thrilling-sweet and rotten
Unforgettable, unforgotten
River-smell, and hear the breeze
Sobbing in the little trees.
Say, do the elm-clumps greatly stand
Still guardians of that holy land?
The chestnuts shade, in reverend dream,
The yet unacademic stream?
Is dawn a secret shy and cold
Anadyomene, silver-gold?
And sunset still a golden sea
From Haslingfield to Madingley?
And after, ere the night is born,
Do hares come out about the corn?
Oh, is the water sweet and cool,
Gentle and brown, above the pool?
And laughs the immortal river still
Under the mill, under the mill?
Say, is there Beauty yet to find?
And Certainty? and Quiet kind?
Deep meadows yet, for to forget
The lies, and truths, and pain? ... oh! yet
Stands the Church clock at ten to three?
And is there honey still for tea?

Bridge of Sighs, Cambridge.

Zennor

ANNE RIDLER

Seen from these cliffs the sea circles slowly,
   Ponderous and blue today, with waves furled,
   Slowly it crosses the curved world.
We wind in its waters with the tide,
   But the pendent ships afar
   Where the lightest blue and low clouds are
We lose as they hover and over the horizon slide.

When it was a dark blue heaven with foam like stars
   We saw it lean above us from the shore,
   And over the rocks the waves rear
Immense, and coming in with crests on fire;
   We could not understand,
   Finding the sea so high above the land,
What held its waters from flooding the world entire.

Today it lies in place, and the dun houses,
   The apple-green cloudy oats, the cows that seem
   Compact of the yellow crust of their cream,
Shrink on Amalveor's grey and tawny sides,
   Sucking the last shreds of sun.
   But all life here is carried on
Against the crash and cry of the moving tides.

St Agnes Head, Cornwall.

Amid the Barren Hills

EMILY BRONTË

There is a spot, 'mid barren hills,
  Where winter howls, and driving rain;
But, if the dreary tempest chills,
  There is a light that warms again.

The house is old, the trees are bare,
  Moonless above bends twilight's dome;
But what on earth is half so dear –
  So longed for – as the hearth of home?

The mute bird sitting on the stone,
  The dank moss dripping from the wall,
The thorn-trees gaunt, the walks o'ergrown,
  I love them – how I love them all! ...

A little and a lone green lane
  That opened on a common wide;
A distant, dreamy, dim blue chain
  Of mountains, circling every side.

A heaven so clear, an earth so calm,
  So sweet, so soft, so hushed an air;
And, deepening still the dream-like charm,
  Wild moor-sheep feeding everywhere.

Farewell

ANNE BRONTË

Farewell to Thee! But not farewell
To all my fondest thoughts of Thee:
Within my heart they still shall dwell
And they shall cheer and comfort me.

Life seems more sweet that Thou didst live
And men more true that Thou wert one:
Nothing is lost that Thou didst give,
Nothing destroyed that Thou hast done.

Opposite: Castle Howard.

Winter in the Fens

John Clare

So moping flat and low our valleys lie,
So dull and muggy is our winter sky,
Drizzling from day to day with threats of rain,
And when that falls still threatening on again;
From one wet week so great an ocean flows
That every village to an island grows,
And every road for even weeks to come
Is stopt, and none but horsemen go from home;
And one wet night leaves travel's best in doubt,
And horseback travellers ask if floods are out
Of every passer-by, and with their horse
The meadow's ocean try in vain to cross;
The horse's footings with a sucking sound
Fill up with water on the firmest ground,
And ruts that dribble into brooks elsewhere
Can find no fall or flat to dribble here,
But filled with wet they brim and overflow
Till hollows in the road to rivers grow;
Then wind with sudden rage, abrupt and blea,
Twirls every lingering leaf from off each tree.
Such is our lowland scene that winter gives,
And strangers wonder where our comfort lives;
Yet in a little close, however keen
The winter comes, I find a patch of green,
Where robins, by the miser winter made
Domestic, flirt and perch upon the spade;
And in a little garden-close at home
I watch for spring – and there's the crocus come!

Tommy

RUDYARD KIPLING

I went into a public-'ouse to get a pint o' beer,
The publican 'e up an' sez 'We serve no red-coats here.'
The girls be'ind the bar they laughed an' giggled fit to die,
I outs into the street again an' to myself sez I:
    O it's Tommy this, an' Tommy that, an' 'Tommy, go away';
    But it's 'Thank you, Mister Atkins,' when the band begins to play–
    The band begins to play, my boys, the band begins to play,
    O it's 'Thank you, Mister Atkins,' when the band begins to play.

I went into a theatre as sober as could be,
They gave a drunk civilian room, but 'adn't none for me;
They sent me to the gallery or round the music-'alls,
But when it comes to fightin', Lord! they'll shove me in the stalls!
    For it's Tommy this, and Tommy that, an' 'Tommy, wait outside';
    But it's 'Special train for Atkins' when the trooper's on the tide–
    The troopship's on the tide, my boys, the troopship's on the tide,
    O it's 'Special train for Atkins' when the trooper's on the tide.

Yes, makin' mock o' uniforms that guard you while you sleep
Is cheaper than them uniforms, an' they're starvation cheap;
An' hustlin' drunken soldiers when they're goin' large a bit
Is five times better business than paradin' in full kit.
    Then it's Tommy this, and Tommy that, an' 'Tommy, 'ow's yer soul?'
    But it's 'Thin red line of 'eroes' when the drums begin to roll–
    The drums begin to roll, my boys, the drums begin to roll,
    O it's 'Thin red line of 'eroes' when the drums begin to roll.

The thin red line.

We aren't no thin red 'eroes, nor we aren't no blackguards too,
But single men in barricks, most remarkable like you;
An' if sometimes our conduck isn't all your fancy paints,
Why, single men in barricks don't grow into plaster saints;
  While it's Tommy this, an' Tommy that, an' 'Tommy, fall be'ind,'
  But it's 'Please to walk in front, sir,' when there's trouble in the wind–
  There's trouble in the wind, my boys, there's trouble in the wind,
  O it's 'Please to walk in front, sir,' when there's trouble in the wind.

You talk o' better food for us, an' schools, an' fires, an' all:
We'll wait for extry rations if you treat us rational.
Don't mess about the cook-room slops, but prove it to our face
The Widow's Uniform is not the soldier-man's disgrace.
  For it's Tommy this, and Tommy that, an' 'Chuck him out, the brute!'
  But it's 'Saviour of 'is country' when the guns begin to shoot;
  An' it's Tommy this, an' Tommy that, an' anything you please;
  An' Tommy ain't a bloomin' fool–you bet that Tommy sees!

Sonnet Composed upon Westminster Bridge

WILLIAM WORDSWORTH

Earth has not anything to show more fair;
Dull would he be of soul who could pass by
A sight so touching in its majesty;
This City now doth, like a garment, wear
The beauty of the morning; silent, bare,
Ships, towers, domes, theatres, and temples lie
Open unto the fields, and to the sky;
All bright and glittering in the smokeless air.
Never did sun more beautifully steep
In his first splendour, valley, rock, or hill;
Ne'er saw I, never felt, a calm so deep!
The river glideth at his own sweet will;
Dear God! the very houses seem asleep;
And all that mighty heart is lying still!

Opposite: Westminster Bridge.

Written at an Inn at Henley

WILLIAM SHENSTONE

To thee, fair freedom! I retire
   From flattery, cards, and dice, and din;
Nor art thou found in mansions higher
   Than the low cot, or humble inn.

'Tis here with boundless power I reign;
   And every health which I begin,
Converts dull port to bright champagne;
   Such freedom crowns it, at an inn.

I fly from pomp, I fly from plate!
   I fly from falsehood's specious grin;
Freedom I love, and form I hate,
   And choose my lodgings at an inn.

Here, waiter! take my sordid ore,
   Which lackeys else might hope to win;
It buys, what courts have not in store;
   It buys me freedom at an inn.

Whoe'er has travelled life's dull round,
   Where'er his stages may have been,
May sigh to think he still has found
   The warmest welcome at an inn.

On the Thames near Goring, Berkshire.

The Passionate Shepherd to his Love

CHRISTOPHER MARLOWE

Come liue with mee and be my loue,
And we will all the pleasure proue,
That hills and valleys, dales and fields,
And all the craggy mountain yeeldes.

There we will sit vpon the Rocks,
And see the sheepheards feede theyr flocks
By shallow riuers, to whose falls
Melodious byrds sing Madrigalls.

And I will make thee beds of Roses,
And a thousand fragrant poesies,
A cap of flowers, and a kirtle,
Imbroydered all with leaues of Mirtle.

A gowne made of the finest wooll,
Which from our pretty Lambes we pull,
Fayre lined slippers for the cold.
With buckles of the purest gold.

A belt of straw and Iuie buds,
With Corall clasps and Amber studs,
And if these pleasures may thee moue,
Come liue with mee, and be my loue.

The sheepheard swains shall daunce and sing
For thy delight each May-morning.
If these delights thy minde may moue,
Then liue with mee, and be my loue.

Opposite: Orchard in springtime.

Sonnet XVIII

William Shakespeare

Shall I compare thee to a summer's day?
Thou art more lovely and more temperate:
Rough winds do shake the darling buds of May,
And summer's lease hath all too short a date:
Sometimes too hot the eye of heaven shines,
And often is his gold complexion dimm'd:
And every fair from fair sometimes declines,
By chance, or nature's changing course untrimm'd;
But thy eternal summer shall not fade,
Nor lose possession of that fair thou ow'st,
Nor shall death brag thou wander'st in his shade,
When in eternal lines to time thou grow'st;
    So long as men can breathe, or eyes can see,
    So long lives this, and this gives life to thee.

In the poppy field.

Sudden Shower

John Clare

Black grows the sudden sky, betokening rain,
    And humming hive-bees homeward hurry by:
They feel the change; so let us shun the grain,
    And take the broad road while our feet are dry.
Aye there, some drops fell moistening on my face,
    And pattering on my hat–'tis coming nigh!–
Let's look about, and find a sheltering place.
    The little things around us fear the sky,
And hasten through the grass to shun the shower.
    Here stoops an ash-tree–hark! the wind gets high,
But never mind; this ivy, for an hour,
    Rain as it may, will keep us drily here:
That little wren knows well his sheltering bower,
    Nor leaves his covert, though we come so near.

Unloading cockles at Wells, Norfolk.

Ode to Autumn

John Keats

Season of mists and mellow fruitfulness,
　Close bosom-friend of the maturing sun;
Conspiring with him how to load and bless
　With fruit the vines that round the thatch-eaves run;
To bend with apples the moss'd cottage-trees,
　And fill all fruit with ripeness to the core;
To swell the gourd, and plump the hazel shells
　With a sweet kernel; to set budding more,
And still more, later flowers for the bees,
　Until they think warm days will never cease;
For Summer has o'erbrimmed their clammy cells.

Who hath not seen Thee oft amid thy store?
　Sometimes whoever seeks abroad may find
Thee sitting careless on a granary floor,
　Thy hair soft-lifted by the winnowing wind;
Or on a half-reap'd furrow sound asleep,
　Drowsed with the fume of poppies, while thy hook
Spares the next swath and all its twinèd flowers;
　And sometimes like a gleaner thou dost keep
Steady thy laden head across a brook;
　Or by a cider-press, with patient look,
Thou watchest the last oozings, hours by hours.

Where are the songs of Spring? Ay, where are they?
　Think not of them, thou hast thy music too,
While barrèd clouds bloom the soft-dying day
　And touch the stubble-plains with rosy hue;
Then in a wailful choir the small gnats mourn
　Among the river-sallows, borne aloft
Or sinking as the light wind lives or dies;
　And full-grown lambs loud bleat from hilly bourn;
Hedge-crickets sing, and now with treble soft
　The redbreast whistles from a garden-croft;
And gathering swallows twitter in the skies.

Opposite: After the harvest.

On Ploughing

Evelyn D Bangay

The slow shuttle of husbandry
Has plodded up and down
Till folds of tilth are lying
In ripples of shining brown.

The slow thoughts of my ancestry
Are moving across my brain.
Turning today's deeds under,
Laying the old facts plain:

How my father strode at his furrowing,
My mother's father spun
And worked in the mills of weaving;
So the image of both is one ...

The plough, horses and harnessing
Weaving slow lines of thread:
My grandfather and my father
Sweating for daily bread.

Opposite: Ploughing with horses.

The Holly

WALTER DE LA MARE

The sturdiest of forest-trees
With acorns is inset;
Wan white blossoms the elder brings
To fruit as black as jet;
But O, in all green English woods
Is aught so fair to view
As the sleek, sharp, dark-leaved holly tree
And its berries burning through?

Towers the ash; and dazzling green
The larch her tassels wears;
Wondrous sweet are the clots of may
The tangled hawthorn bears;
But O, in heath or meadow or wold
Springs aught beneath the blue
As brisk and trim as a holly-tree bole
With its berries burning through?

When hither, thither, falls the snow,
And blazes small the frost,
Naked amid the winter stars
The elm's vast boughs are tossed;
But O, of all that summer showed
What now to winter's true
As the prickle-beribbed dark holly tree,
With its berries burning through!

Holly at Christmas.

The Oxen

Thomas Hardy

Christmas Eve, and twelve of the clock.
　'Now they are all on their knees,'
An elder said as we sat in a flock
　By the embers in hearthside ease.

We pictured the meek mild creatures where
　They dwelt in their strawy pen,
Nor did it occur to one of us there
　To doubt they were kneeling then.

So fair a fancy few would weave
　In these years! Yet, I feel
If someone said on Christmas Eve,
　'Come; see the oxen kneel

'In the lonely barton by yonder coomb
　Our childhood used to know,'
I should go with him in the gloom,
　Hoping it might be so.

Opposite: Silhouettes and shadows.

From *The Burning of Leaves*

LAURENCE BINYON

Now is the time for the burning of the leaves.
They go to the fire, the nostril pricks with smoke
Wandering slowly into a weeping mist.
Brittle and blotched, ragged and rotten sheaves!
A flame seizes the smouldering ruin and bites
On stubborn stalks that crackle as they resist.

The last hollyhock's fallen tower is dust:
All the spices of June are a bitter reek.
All the extravagant riches spent and mean.
All burns! The reddest rose is a ghost;
Sparks whirl up, to expire in the mist: the wild
Fingers of fire are making corruption clean.

Now is the time for stripping the spirit bare,
Time for the burning of days ended and done.
Idle solace of things that have gone before.
Rootless hope and fruitless desire are there:
Let them go to the fire with never a look behind.
The world that was ours is a world that is ours no more.

They will come again, the leaf and the flower, to arise
From squalor of rottenness into the old splendour.
And magical scents to a wondering memory bring
The same glory, to shine upon different eyes.
Earth cares for her own ruins, naught for ours.
Nothing is certain, only the certain spring.

Tending the bonfire

Diary of a Church Mouse

JOHN BETJEMAN

Here among long-discarded cassocks,
Damp stools, and half-split open hassocks.
Here where the Vicar never looks
I nibble through old service books.
Lean and alone I spend my days
Behind this Church of England baize.
I share my dark forgotten room
With two oil-lamps and half a broom.
The cleaner never bothers me,
So here I eat my frugal tea.
My bread is sawdust mixed with straw;
My jam is polish for the floor.

      Christmas and Easter may be feasts
For congregations and for priests.
And so may Whitsun. All the same,
They do not fill my meagre frame.
For me the only feast at all
Is Autumn's Harvest Festival,
When I can satisfy my want
With ears of corn around the font.

I climb the eagle's brazen head
To burrow through a loaf of bread.
I scramble up the pulpit stair
And gnaw the marrows hanging there.

      It is enjoyable to taste
These items ere they go to waste.
But how annoying when one finds
That other mice with pagan minds
Come into church my food to share
Who have no proper business there.
Two field mice who have no desire
To be baptized, invade the choir.
A large and most unfriendly rat
Comes in to see what we are at.
He says he thinks there is no God
And yet he comes ... it's rather odd.
This year he stole a sheaf of wheat
(It screened our special preacher's seat).
And prosperous mice from fields away
Come in to hear the organ play.
And under cover of its notes
Eat through the altar's sheaf of oats.

A Low Church mouse, who thinks that I
Am too papistical, and High
Yet somehow doesn't think it wrong
To munch through Harvest Evensong.
While I, who starve the whole year through,
Must share my food with rodents who
Except at this time of the year
Not once inside the church appear.

      Within the human world I know
Such goings-on could not be so.
For human beings only do
What their religion tells them to.
They read the Bible every day
And always, night and morning, pray,
And just like me, the good church mouse,
Worship each week in God's own house.

      But all the same it's strange to me
How very full the church can be
With people I don't see at all
Except at Harvest Festival.

Selworthy Church, Somerset.

From Miss Thompson Goes Shopping

Martin Armstrong

In her lone cottage on the downs,
With winds and blizzards and great crowns
Of shining cloud, with wheeling plover
And short grass sweet with the small white clover,
Miss Thompson lived, correct and meek.
A lonely spinster, and every week
On market-day she used to go
Into the little town below,
Tucked in the great downs' hollow bowl,
Like pebbles gathered in a shoal.

So, having washed her plates and cup
And banked the kitchen fire up,
Miss Thompson slipped upstairs and dressed.
Put on her black (her second best),
The bonnet trimmed with rusty plush.
Peeped in the glass with simpering blush.
From camphor-smelling cupboard took
Her thicker jacket off the hook
Because the day might turn to cold.
Then, ready, slipped downstairs and rolled
The hearthrug back: then searched about.
Found her basket, ventured out.
Snecked the door and paused to lock it
And plunged the key in some deep pocket.

Then as she tripped demurely down
The steep descent, the little town
Spread wider till its sprawling street
Enclosed her and her footfalls beat
On hard stone pavement: and she felt
Those throbbing ecstasies that melt
Through heart and mind, as, happy, free,
Her small, prim personality
Merged into the seething strife
Of auction-marts and city life.

Anticipation outside a cake shop, Lincoln.

98

If I Could Tell You

W H Auden

Time will say nothing but I told you so.
Time only knows the price we have to pay:
If I could tell you I would let you know.

If we should weep when clowns put on their show,
If we should stumble when musicians play,
Time will say nothing but I told you so.

There are no fortunes to be told, although,
Because I love you more than I can say,
If I could tell you I would let you know.

The winds must come from somewhere when they blow,
There must be reasons why the leaves decay;
Time will say nothing but I told you so.

Perhaps the roses really want to grow,
The vision seriously intends to stay;
If I could tell you I would let you know.

Suppose the lions all get up and go,
And all the brooks and soldiers run away;
Will Time say nothing but I told you so?
If I could tell you I would let you know.

Opposite: In the bleak midwinter.

Oxford

Tom Lovatt-Williams

I see the coloured lilacs flame
In many an ancient Oxford lane
And bright laburnum holds its bloom
Suspended golden in the noon.
The placid lawns I often tread
Are stained and carpeted with red
Where the tall chestnuts cast their flowers
To make the fleeting April hours,
And now the crowded hawthorn yields
Its haunting perfume to the fields
With men and maidens hurrying out
Along Port Meadow to the Trout.
There, by the coruscating stream
To drink and gaze and gaze and dream:
An ageless dame leaves her abode
To caper down the Woodstock Road
And greet a Dean she used to know
A trifling sixty years ago.
Queer tricycles of unknown date
Are pedalled at a frightful rate
Their baskets bulge with borrowed books
Or terriers of uncertain looks.

Perpetual motion in The High
Beneath a blue and primrose sky
And cherry blossom like a cloud
Beside the traffic roaring loud,
While daffodils go dancing gold
In streets where time runs grey and old
And poets, sweating in the throng,
Can sometimes hear a blackbird's song.
All Oxford's spires are tipped with rose
A wind full magic sweetly blows
And suddenly it seems in truth
As if the centuries of youth
Are crowding all the streets and lanes
In April when the lilac flames.

The High, Oxford.

Roundabouts and Swings

PATRICK R CHALMERS

It was early last September nigh to Framlin'am-on-Sea,
An' 'twas Fair-day come to-morrow, an' the time was after tea.
An' I met a painted caravan adown a dusty lane,
A Pharaoh with his waggons comin' jolt an' creak an' strain;
A cheery cove an' sunburnt, bolt o' eye and wrinkled up.
An' beside him on the splashboard sat a brindled terrier pup,
An' a lurcher wise as Solomon an' lean as fiddle-strings
Was joggin' in the dust along 'is roundabouts and swings.

'Goo'-day,' said 'e: 'Goo'-day,' said I: 'an' 'ow d'you find things go,
An' what's the chance o' millions when you runs a travellin' show?'
"I find,' said 'e, 'things very much as 'ow I've always found,
For mostly they goes up and down or else goes round and round.'
Said 'e, 'The job's the very spit o' what it always were,
It's bread and bacon mostly when the dog
   don't catch a 'are:
But lookin' at it broad, an' while it ain't no
   merchant king's,
What's lost upon the roundabouts we
   pulls up on the swings!'

'Goo' luck,' said 'e: 'Goo' luck,' said I: 'you've put it past a doubt:
An' keep that lurcher on the road, the gamekeepers is out':
'E thumped upon the footboard an' 'e lumbered on again
To meet a gold-dust sunset down the owl-light in the lane:
An' the moon she climbed the 'azels, while a nightjar seemed to spin
That Pharaoh's wisdom o'er again, 'is sooth of lose-and-win:
For 'up an' down an' round,' said 'e, 'goes all appointed things,
An' losses on the roundabouts means profits on the swings!'

A giant of yesterday.

The Glory of the Garden

RUDYARD KIPLING

Our England is a garden that is full of stately views.
Of borders, beds and shrubberies and lawns and avenues.
With statues on the terraces and peacocks strutting by;
But the Glory of the Garden lies in more than meets the eye.

For where the old thick laurels grow, along the thin red wall,
You find the tool- and potting-sheds which are the heart of all;
The cold-frames and the hot-houses, the dungpits and the tanks,
The rollers, carts and drain-pipes, with the barrows and the planks.

And there you'll see the gardeners, the men and 'prentice boys
Told off to do as they are bid and do it without noise;
For, except when seeds are planted and we shout to scare the birds,
The Glory of the Garden it abideth not in words.

And some can pot begonias and some can bud a rose,
And some are hardly fit to trust with anything that grows;
But they can roll and trim the lawns and sift the sand and loam.
For the Glory of the Garden occupieth all who come.

Our England is a garden, and such gardens are not made
By singing:–'Oh, how beautiful!' and sitting in the shade,
While better men than we go out and start their working lives
At grubbing weeds from gravel-paths with broken dinner-knives.

There's not a pair of legs so thin, there's not a head so thick,
There's not a hand so weak and white, nor yet a heart so sick,
But it can find some needful job that's crying to be done,
For the Glory of the Garden glorifieth every one.

Then seek your job with thankfulness and work till further orders.
If it's only netting strawberries or killing slugs on borders:
And when your back stops aching and your hands begin to harden,
You will find yourself a partner in the Glory of the Garden.

Oh, Adam was a gardener, and God who made him sees
That half a proper gardener's work is done upon his knees.
So when your work is finished, you can wash your hands and pray
For the Glory of the Garden, that it may not pass away!
And the Glory of the Garden it shall never pass away!

Stone House garden, Worcestershire.

The Ruined Maid

Thomas Hardy

'O 'Melia, my dear, this does everything crown!
Who could have supposed I should meet you in Town?
And whence such fair garments, such prosperi-ty?'–
'O didn't you know I'd been ruined?' said she.

–'You left us in tatters, without shoes or socks,
Tired of digging potatoes, and spudding up docks;
And now you've gay bracelets and bright feathers three!'–
'Yes: that's how we dress when we're ruined,' said she.

–'At home in the barton you said "thee" and "thou,"
And "thik oon," and "theäs oon," and "t'other"; but now
Your talking quite fits 'ee for high compa-ny!'–
'Some polish is gained with one's ruin,' said she.

–'Your hands were like paws then, your face blue and bleak
But now I'm bewitched by your delicate cheek,
And your little gloves fit as on any la-dy!'–
'We never do work when we're ruined,' said she.

–'You used to call home-life a hag-ridden dream,
And you'd sigh, and you'd sock; but at present you seem
To know not of megrims or melancho-ly!'–
'True. One's pretty lively when ruined,' said she.

–'I wish I had feathers, a fine sweeping gown,
And a delicate face, and could strut about Town!'–
'My dear–a raw country girl, such as you be,
Cannot quite expect that. You ain't ruined,' said she.

York: The Traditional English Tearooms.

TEA·ROOMS AND COFFEE·SHOP

CAFE MENU

TAYLORS

TEA·ROOMS

46

CAFE MENU

The Life That I Have

Leo Marks

The life that I have
Is all that I have
And the life that I have
Is yours

The love that I have
Of the life that I have
Is yours and yours and yours

A sleep I shall have
A rest I shall have
Yet death will be but a pause

For the peace of my years
In the long green grass
Will be yours and yours and yours

Sunset.

The Gate of the Year

M Louise Haskins

And I said to the man who stood at the
  gate of the year:
'Give me a light, that I may tread safely
  into the unknown!'
And he replied
'Go out into the darkness and put your
  hand into the Hand of God.
That shall be to you better than light
  and safer than a known way.'

So, I went forth, and finding the Hand
  of God, trod gladly into the night
And He led me toward the hills and
  the breaking of day in the lone East

So, heart, be still!
What need our little life,
Our human life, to know,
If God hath comprehension?
In all the dizzy strife
Of things both high and low
God hideth His intention

Peterborough Cathedral.

Dovecotes at Naunton, Gloucestershire, left, and Eardisland, Herefordshire, right.

Take time to stop and wonder…

Enjoying the spectacular view from Yat Rock, Forest of Dean.

This volume is benefiting a wide range of charities throughout England. We do hope you enjoy the poems and pictures and that they will serve as a constant reminder of England's rich heritage, time and time again through the years.

Index of first lines

Page

113 And I said to the man who stood at the gate of the year:

62 Be not afeard: the isle is full of noises,

54 Before the Roman came to Rye or out to Severn strode,

53 Beside a runnel build my shed,

84 Black grows the sudden sky, betokening rain,

92 Christmas Eve, and twelve of the clock.

80 Come liue with mee and be my loue,

42 Coombe and Tor, green meadow and lane,

76 Earth has not anything to show more fair;

70 Farewell to Thee! But not farewell

50 Happy the man, whose wish and care

97 Here among long-discarded cassocks,

15 How stately stand yon pines upon the hill,

20 I come from haunts of coot and hern,

40 I have made tales in verse, but this man made

60 I must go down to the seas again, to the lonely sea and the sky,

46 I remember, I remember

102 I see the coloured lilacs flame

10 I wandered lonely as a cloud

74 I went into a public-'ouse to get a pint o' beer,

48 If I should die think only this of me:

34 If this country were a sea (that is solid rock

45 If you can keep your head when all about you

98 In her lone cottage on the downs,

56 In summertime on Bredon

104 It was early last September nigh to Framlin'am-on-Sea,

Page

64 Just now the lilac is in bloom,

22 Loveliest of trees, the cherry now

59 Miss J Hunter Dunn, Miss J Hunter Dunn,

94 Now is the time for the burning of the leaves.

38 O blithe New-comer! I have heard,

108 'O 'Melia, my dear, this does everything crown!

18 Oh, to be in England,

24 Once more unto the breach, dear friends, once more;

36 'One day, one day, I'll climb that distant hill

106 Our England is a garden that is full of stately views.

86 Season of mists and mellow fruitfulness,

68 Seen from these cliffs the sea circles slowly,

82 Shall I compare thee to a summer's day?

72 So moping flat and low our valleys lie,

26 The curfew tolls the knell of parting day,

111 The life that I have

88 The slow shuttle of husbandry

91 The sturdiest of forest-trees

70 There is a spot, 'mid barren hills,

16 This is the weather the cuckoo likes,

8 This royal throne of kings, this scepter'd isle,

100 Time will say nothing but I told you so.

78 To thee, fair freedom! I retire

12 Up on the downs the red-eyed kestrels hover,

32 We used to picnic where the thrift

30 Yes, I remember Adlestrop –

Olchon Valley, Herefordshire

Arrow Valley Publications

Arrow Valley Publications
is in the centre of the beautiful medieval village
of Eardisland in north Herefordshire.
The placid River Arrow winds between
well tended gardens: from our office windows
we look through the shrubs and trees of
our garden to the great stone tower
of our Norman church.
Eardisland is a classic English village…
timeless but full of quiet purposeful activity:
it is enjoyed by thousands of visitors each year,
from all over the world.

Having lived in this delightful setting
for thirty years, Kathleen and Barry Freeman
formed Arrow Valley Publications early in 1999,
to create beautiful books about England and,
in the process, to generate funds for a range
of charities. Their first book, *The Spirit of
Herefordshire 2000*, was published as a limited
edition casebound volume in April 2000.
It raised £1250 for four Herefordshire charities:
St Michael's Hospice; Hereford Cathedral;
Herefordshire Historic Churches and
Herefordshire Nature Trust.

This book was also published in
a soft cover edition, and is now available by post:
please see opposite page.

The view from Arrow Valley Publications office windows.

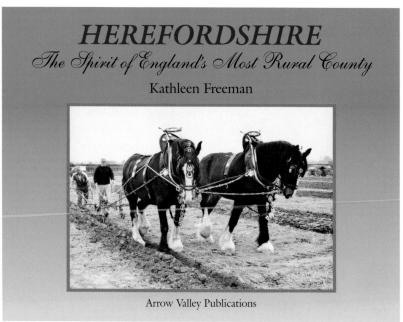